CW00587867

The Joys of Christmas

The Joys of Christmas

A COLLECTION OF THOUGHTS,
IDEAS AND RECIPES FOR THE
FESTIVE SEASON

COMPILED BY
MARIAN FRENCH

ILLUSTRATED BY
JUDY BENJAMIN

EBURY
PRESS

First published in Great Britain 1990 by Ebury Press
an imprint of the Random Century Group
Random Century House
20 Vauxhall Bridge Road
London SW1V 2SA

by arrangement with Bow Press
208 Victoria Road
Drummoyne, NSW 2047
Australia

A CIP catalogue record is available from the British Library.

ISBN 0 85223 950 5

Designed by Maree Cunningham
Calligraphy by Margrit Eisenmann

Typeset by Excel Imaging Pty Ltd, Sydney
Printed in Singapore by Tien Wah
Production by Vantage Graphics

Introduction

*C*hristmas means . . . children, family, cards and mince pies; kissing under mistletoe, music and myrrh, puddings and jelly beans, candy and toys, almonds, angels and gingerbread cookies, lumpy Christmas stockings and three wise men; dolls, drums, ham and holly, Santa Claus, walnuts, reindeer and turkey; carols and candles, jingle bells, fruitcake, gold, garlands and gifts . . . but most of all Christmas means love. The ways in which we celebrate may differ, but its spirit will always remain – the spirit of sharing and giving, of well wishing and warmth.

Family Plum Pudding

250g (8oz) RAISINS
250g (8oz) SULTANAS
125g (4oz) CURRANTS
60g (2oz) MIXED PEEL
60g (2oz) BLANCHED
  ALMONDS CHOPPED
250g (8oz) BUTTER
250g (8oz) BROWN SUGAR
250g (8oz) SOFT, WHITE
  BREADCRUMBS

125ml (4 fl oz) BRANDY OR
  DARK RUM
150g (5oz) PLAIN FLOUR
PINCH SALT
1 TEASPOON MIXED
  SPICE
½ TEASPOON
  BICARBONATE
  OF SODA
1 TEASPOON NUTMEG
4 EGGS

1. Chop raisins and mix with sultanas, currants, peel and almonds
2. Cream butter and sugar until light and fluffy and add eggs one at a time, beating well after each addition.
3. Stir in fruits and brandy.
4. Sift together flour, salt, spice, soda and nutmeg. Add to creamed mixture with breadcrumbs, mixing well. Spoon into well-greased, 2 litre (3½ pint) pudding basin.
5. Cover securely with 2 layers of greased aluminium foil or a snap-on lid. Place on trivet or old plate in a large saucepan with sufficient boiling water to come two-thirds of the way up the sides of the basin. Cover the saucepan and boil gently but steadily for five hours, replacing boiling water as necessary. Store pudding in the refrigerator and re-steam for two hours on day of serving.

Little Jack Horner
Sat in a corner
Eating his Christmas pie.
He put in his thumb
And pulled out a plum,
And said what a good boy am I.

Brandy Butter

185g (6oz) BUTTER   60ml (2 fl oz) BRANDY
125g (4oz) CASTOR SUGAR

*C*ream butter with sugar until light and fluffy.
Gradually beat in brandy a little at a time.
Pour into container and allow to harden. May be
covered and stored in refrigerator until ready
for use.

Pudding Charms

Our Christmas pudding was made in November. All they put in it, I quite well remember: Currants and raisins, sugar and spice, Orange peel, lemon peel – everything nice.

CHARLOTTE DRUID COLE

Christmas is coming,
The geese are getting fat,
Please to put a penny
In the old man's hat;
If you haven't got a penny,
A ha'penny will do,
If you haven't got a ha'penny,
Then God bless you!

BEGGAR'S RHYME

Christmas time! That man must be a misanthrope indeed, in whose breast something like a jovial feeling is not roused – in whose mind some pleasant associations are not awakened – by the recurrence of Christmas. . . . Would that Christmas lasted the whole year through (as it ought) and that the prejudices and passions which deform our better nature were never called into action among those to whom they should ever be strangers!

CHARLES DICKENS, *Sketches by Boz*, 1836

Most all the time, the whole year round, there
   ain't no flies on me,
But jest 'fore Christmas I'm as good as I kin be!
                    EUGENE FIELD, *Jest 'Fore Christmas*

Some say that ever 'gainst that season come,
Wherein our Saviour's birth is celebrated,
The bird of dawning singeth all night long;
And then they say, no spirit dare walk abroad.
The nights are wholesome; then no planets strike,
No fairy takes, nor witch has power to charm —
So hallowed and so gracious is the time.
                    WILLIAM SHAKESPEARE, *Hamlet*

Glad Christmas comes, and every hearth
Makes room to bid him welcome now . . .
                    JOHN CLARE

A little child,
 a shining star,
A stable rude,
 the door ajar.
Yet in that place
 so crude, forlorn,
The Hope of all the
 world was born.

ANONYMOUS

It came upon the midnight clear,
That glorious song of old,
From angels bending near the earth
To touch their harps of gold;
"Peace on the earth, good will to men
From Heaven's all-gracious King" —
The world in solemn stillness lay
To hear the angels sing.

E.H. SEARS, *Christmas Carol*, 1850

For Christ is born of Mary,
And gathered all above,
While mortals sleep, the angels keep
Their watch of wond'ring love.
O morning stars, together
Proclaim the holy birth!
And praises sing to God the King,
And peace to men on earth!

PHILLIPS BROOKS,
O Little Town of Bethlehem, 1868

God rest ye, little children; let nothing you
      affright,
For Jesus Christ, your Saviour, was born this
      happy night;
Along the hills of Galilee the white flocks
      sleeping lay,
When Christ, the Child of Nazareth, was
      born on Christmas day.

DIANA MULOCK CRAIK, *Christmas Carol*, 1881

The time draws near the birth of Christ:
The moon is hid; the night is still;
The Christmas bells from hill to hill
Answer each other in the mist.
      ALFRED TENNYSON, *In Memoriam, XXVIII*, 1850

The hour in which the Prince of Peace was born.
      WILLIAM CULLEN BRYANT

I heard the bells on Christmas day
Their old familiar carols play,
    And wild and sweet
    The words repeat
Of "Peace on earth, good will to men!"
      HENRY WADSWORTH LONGFELLOW

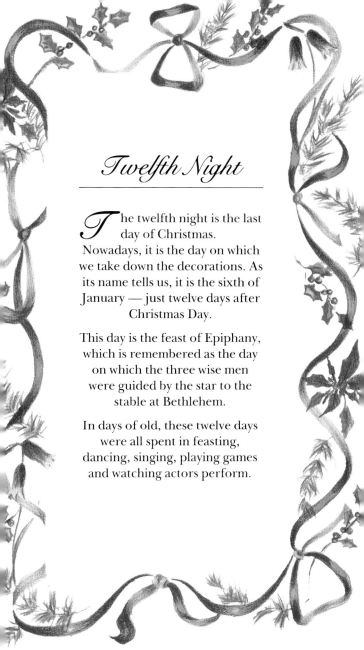

Twelfth Night

*T*he twelfth night is the last day of Christmas. Nowadays, it is the day on which we take down the decorations. As its name tells us, it is the sixth of January — just twelve days after Christmas Day.

This day is the feast of Epiphany, which is remembered as the day on which the three wise men were guided by the star to the stable at Bethlehem.

In days of old, these twelve days were all spent in feasting, dancing, singing, playing games and watching actors perform.

Boughs of Green

A welcome touch of holly: the combination of dried holly leaves, mountain daisies, imitation crab-apples and gypsophila makes a superb wreath for your entrance door. A big jug of gypsophila inside the front door adds to the Christmas spirit of your house.

Requirements: Foam wreath base, florist ribbon and red and green wire, Christmas decorations, Santa, Holly spray baubles.

Collect grasses and dry, hanging heads down to use in dried arrangements. For lovely Christmas door decorations, tie in a sheaf with a wide red or tartan ribbon.

In countries where the earth is blanketed in snow in mid-winter and the trees are bare, evergreens are a sign of continuing life.
The holly has always been a symbol of fertility. The green of its leaves and the red of its berries became the colours of Christmas.

In the southern hemisphere, Christmas is a time of fruit and flowers, so evergreens lose their special significance. In New Zealand the red pohutakawa blossom is the flower of Christmas, Australia has the flowering Christmas Bush and Christmas bells. The poinsettia is another popular Christmas flower all over the world.

It is Christmas
   in the mansion,
Yule-log fires
   and silken frocks;
It is Christmas
   in the cottage,
Mother's filling
   little socks.

ANONYMOUS

18

Rum Balls

*T*hese make an especially festive gift packaged in small square acetate boxes and tied with tartan ribbon.

1 pkt PLAIN BISCUITS,
   CRUMBED
60g (2oz) WALNUTS,
   FINELY CHOPPED
2 TABLESPOONS COCOA

80ml (3 fl oz) LIQUID
   GLUCOSE
60ml (2 fl oz) RUM
CHOCOLATE SPRINKLES

1. Blend crumbs, walnuts and cocoa, then add glucose and rum, mixing well.
2. Form the mixture into small balls by rolling them smooth in the palms of you hands, which should be moistened to prevent sticking.
3. Toss the balls in chocolate sprinkles, chill until firm. Allow to mature for a few days.

Come, bring with a noise,
My merrie, merrie boyes,
The Christmas log to the firing;
While my good Dame, she
Bids ye all be free;
And drink to your hearts desiring.

Drink now the strong Beere,
Cut the white loafe here,
The while the meat is a-shredding;
For the rare Mince-Pie
And the Plums stand by
To fill the paste that's a-kneading.

ROBERT HERRICK, *The Yule Log*

Yule Log Burn
Joy Joy
God Give us Joy
Christmas has arrived.

For they said it was a shame to quarrel upon
Christmas Day. And so it was! God love it,
so it was.

CHARLES DICKENS, *A Christmas Carol*

Wisselton, wasselton, who lives here?
We've come to taste your Christmas beer.
Up the kitchen and down the hall,
Holly, ivy and mistletoe;
A peck of apples will serve us all,
Give us some apples and let us go.

TRADITIONAL

Make we merry, both more and less,
For now is the time of Christmas!
If that he say he cannot sing,
Some other sport then let him bring.
That it may please at this feasting
For now is the time of Christmas

WALTER DE LA MARE

These holidays we'll briskly drink
All mirth we will devise,
No Treason will we speak or think;
Then bring up the brave minc'd pies,
Roast Beef and brave Plum-porridge,
Our Loyal hearts to chear, (sic)
Then prithee make no more ado,
But bring up Christmas beer.

ANONYMOUS

Carols

Carols instantly evoke the mood of Christmas for all those who hear them. The word "carol" has a disputed history, but it probably comes from the Old French term for a ring dance. The first carols were sung by the angels at Christ's nativity, but they did not become popular in England until the fourteenth century.

Joy to the world! the Lord is come;
Let earth receive her King;
Let every heart prepare him room,
And heaven and nature sing,
And heaven and nature sing,
And heaven, and heaven and nature sing.

We three kings of Orient are.
Bearing gifts we traverse afar.
Field and fountain, moor and mountain
Following yonder star.

Silent night, holy night.
All is calm, all is bright.
Round yon Virgin Mother and Child,
Holy Infant so tender and mild,
Sleep in Heavenly peace,
Sleep in Heavenly peace.

Hark! the herald angels sing,
Glory to the new-born King;
Peace on earth and mercy mild,
God and sinners reconciled.
Joyful all ye nations rise,
Join the triumph of the skies,
With th'angelic host proclaim:
"Christ is born in Bethlehem".

Jingle bells, jingle bells,
Jingle all the way,
O! what fun it is to ride,
On a one-horse open sleigh.

To Mary, rose of heaven,
With loving hearts we say
Let our sins be forgiven,
And grief be turned away
Upon this Christmas Day:
To Jesus, Child of Winter,
For grace and hope we pray.

The holly and the ivy, now both are well
full grown,
Of all the trees that are in the wood, the
holly bears the crown,
The rising of the sun, and the running of
the deer,
The playing of the merry organ, sweet
singing in the choir.

The holly bears a prickle, as sharp as any thorn,
And Mary bore sweet Jesus Christ, on
Christmas Day in the morn.

Mulled Wine

$\mathscr{I}$t is an old tradition to serve carolling groups hot mulled cider or wine.

Pour bottle of cider into a heavy saucepan and toss in 4 or 5 cloves. As it heats, add ¼ teaspoon of cinnamon, 2 teaspoons of honey and several slices of orange and lemon. Make it very hot but do not let it boil. When serving, sprinkle a little nutmeg on top.

Santa Claus

On Christmas Eve all over the world children hang their stockings and eagerly await the arrival of Santa Clause.

Children of European countries would find presents left to them by the good Saint Nicholas, while in America children were left gifts by someone who was as kind as St. Nicholas. He was called Santa Claus.

Endowed with extraordinary powers, he is without human limitations, is able to circum-navigate the globe in one single night and has no difficulty in being in countless places at one time.

Known as Father Christmas to the English, Pére Noël to the French, Sinterclaus to the Dutch. The Germans call him Christkindl. The Chinese have their Lam Khoong Khoong, meaning Nice Old Father, and the Japanese have Hoteisho, who has eyes in both the back and front of his head and carries a big bag of toys. On Epiphany Eve in Italy the good little witch Befana comes down the chimney on a broom and fills the shoes of good Italian boys and girls with toys. Those who have not been good could find their shoes filled with charcoal and ash.

Bring forth the fir tree,
The box and the bay,
Deck out our cottage
For glad Christmas Day.

ANONYMOUS

O Christmas tree, O Christmas tree,
Thy leaves are green forever.
O Christmas tree, O Christmas tree,
Thy beauty leaves thee never.
Thy leaves are green in summer's prime,
Thy leaves are green at Christmas time.
O Christmas tree, O Christmas tree,
Thy leaves are green forever.

GERMAN CHRISTMAS CAROL

Resplendent stands
the glitt'ring tree
Weighted with gifts
for all to see.

ANNE P.L. FIELD

31

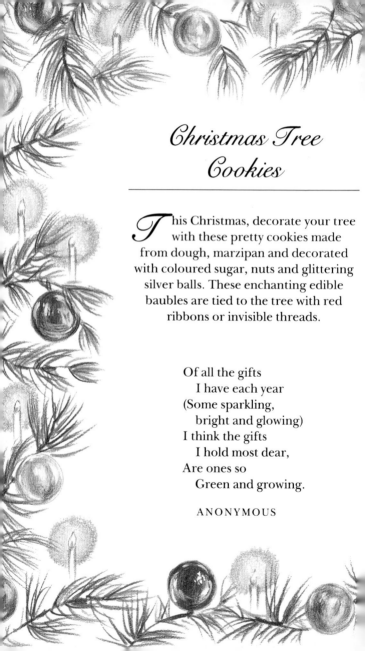

Christmas Tree Cookies

*T*his Christmas, decorate your tree with these pretty cookies made from dough, marzipan and decorated with coloured sugar, nuts and glittering silver balls. These enchanting edible baubles are tied to the tree with red ribbons or invisible threads.

Of all the gifts
   I have each year
(Some sparkling,
   bright and glowing)
I think the gifts
   I hold most dear,
Are ones so
   Green and growing.

ANONYMOUS

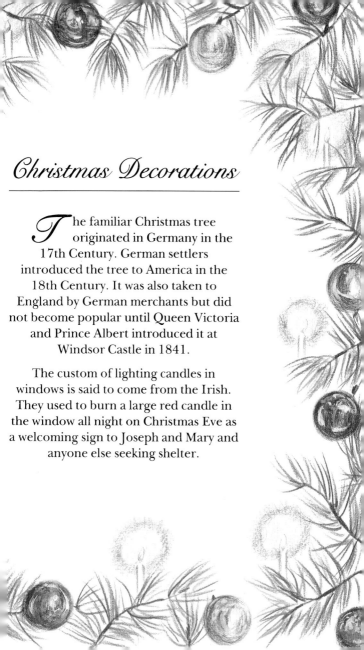

Christmas Decorations

*T*he familiar Christmas tree originated in Germany in the 17th Century. German settlers introduced the tree to America in the 18th Century. It was also taken to England by German merchants but did not become popular until Queen Victoria and Prince Albert introduced it at Windsor Castle in 1841.

The custom of lighting candles in windows is said to come from the Irish. They used to burn a large red candle in the window all night on Christmas Eve as a welcoming sign to Joseph and Mary and anyone else seeking shelter.

Disguise and Fancy Dress

*F*rom the Roman celebrations of Saturnalia and Kalends, to the tradition of star singers and mumming, Victorian pantomime and parlour games, dressing up has played an essential part in mid-winter (Christmas) festivities. Costumes can be elaborate or impromptu affairs.

Games

BLIND MAN'S BLUFF

*T*his game was reportedly played as long ago as the middle of the sixteenth century during the twelve days of Christmas.

Blindfold a player with a scarf then spin them round three times. They must then wander round the room trying to catch someone. If they do, they must guess who it is. If they guess correctly, that player becomes the Blind Man, if not they must continue.

CHARADES

*P*layed at Christmas in Victorian England.

Divide into two teams, each team selects a word which the other team must mime, etc.

'Twas the night before Christmas, when all
   through the house,
Not a creature was stirring, not even a mouse;
The stockings were hung by the chimney with
   care
In hopes that St Nicholas soon would be there.

   CLEMENT C. MOORE, *A Visit from St Nicholas*

Fine old Christmas, with the snowy hair and
ruddy face, had done his duty that year in the
noblest fashion, and had set off his rich gifts of
warmth and colour with all the heightening
contrast of frost and snow.

   GEORGE ELIOT, *The Mill on the Floss*

At Christmas play, and make good cheer,
   For Christmas comes but once a year.

THOMAS TUSSER,
*Five Hundred Points of
Good Husbandry*, 1580

But I heard him exclaim, 'ere he drove out
   of sight,
"Happy Christmas to all, and to all a good-night."

CLEMENT CLARK MOORE

Bread Stuffing

*I*n the warm and busy kitchens of New England children always shared in making the seasoning for the roasted bird. Using leftover ends of bread, onions, herbs from the garden – sage, lovage, marjoram and thyme – the children prepared the stuffing, seasoning it with salt and pepper.

Bread Sauce For Poultry

*B*oil an onion in 600ml (1 pint) of milk till tender. Strain the milk over 150g (6oz) of soft breadcrumbs (leaving out the onion). Let it stand near heat for about an hour, then beat up, smooth and season with nutmeg, pepper and salt.

Caviar, Toast and Lemon

B uy the best grade of caviar you can. Serve it in a glass bowl placed in another bowl full of chopped ice, or if you prefer, use a silver bowl. Place lemon wedges and toast alongside.

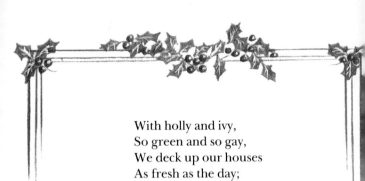

With holly and ivy,
So green and so gay,
We deck up our houses
As fresh as the day;

With bay and rosemary
And laurel complete;
And every one now
Is a king in conceit.

But give me holly,
  bold and jolly
Honest, prickly, shining holly;
Pluck me holly leaf and berry
For the day when I make merry.

CHRISTINA ROSSETTI

Sitting under the mistletoe
(Pale green, fairy mistletoe)
One last candle burning low,
All the sleepy dancers gone,
Just one candle burning on.
Shadows lurking everywhere:
Someone came, and kissed me there

WALTER DE LA MARE

MISTLETOE
The all-healer and plant of peace, it induces
fertility, banishes evil spirits and protects homes
against thunder and lightning.

HOLLY
Protection against witches and the evil eye.
Symbolic of the burning bush in which God
appeared to Moses and Christ's crown of thorns.

IVY
The sacred plant of Bacchus, believed to protect
against drunkenness

Christmas Stockings

*I*n early Victorian days of the nineteenth-century England, hanging stockings from the mantlepiece or bedpost became a custom. St. Nicholas used to ride from Spain on a horse and put presents in clogs and wooden shoes. Leather laced shoes could not easily be filled so English and American children hung up their stockings instead. As both boys and girls wore long heavy cotton and wool socks over their knees, there was plenty of length to hold goodies. There was always a small new coin on the toe, followed by an orange, the first a symbol of wealth and the second a symbol of the return of the sun the coming year.

Home crafted 'stockings' can also be made in the shape of Santa Claus's boots, cut from bright sturdy materials, white or coloured felt and trimmed with braid or ribbons, decorated with sequins, tiny bells and tufts of cotton wool.

Merry Christmas Cookies

For bells, stockings, stars, wreaths, etc

Mix thoroughly
75g (3oz) SOFTENED
  BUTTER
75g (3oz) SUGAR
1 EGG
225g (8oz) HONEY
1 TEASPOON LEMON
  FLAVORING

Sift together and stir in
400g (14oz) PLAIN FLOUR
1 TEASPOON BICARB
  SODA
1 TEASPOON SALT

*C*hill dough. Roll out ¼ inch or 50mm thick. Cut into desired shapes with biscuit cutter. Press a paper clip into the back of biscuit for hanging. Place well-spaced on lightly greased baking sheet. Bake at 375°F, 200°C or gas mark 5 for 8 to 10 minutes.

Please remember to remove the paperclip from the biscuit before giving to small children, and hang the biscuit out of their reach to prevent accidents.

Glorious time of great Too-Much.

LEIGH HUNT

Christmas itself may be called into question
If carried so far it creates indigestion.

RALPH BERGENGREN, *The Unwise Christmas*

Call a truce, then, to our labours — let us feast
   with friends and neighbours,
And be merry as the custom of our caste;
For if "faint and forced the laughter", and if
   sadness follow after,
We are richer by one mocking Christmas past.

RUDYARD KIPLING, *Christmas in India*, 1886

Bounce, buckram, velvet's dear,
Christmas comes but once a year;
And when it comes, it brings good cheer,
But when it's gone it's never near.

He's as busy as an English oven at Christmas.

ITALIAN SAYING

May thy Christmas
   happy be,
And naught
   but joy appear,
Is now the wish
   I send to thee,
And all I love
   most dear.

VERSE ON A VICTORIAN CHRISTMAS CARD

The orange has
its place
you know,
To fill each
Christmas
stocking toe.

ROSEANNE RUSSELL

Potpourri

*H*ere is a delightful potpourri for Christmas. Place a bowl on the hearth near the warmth of your fire to bring out the rich spicy fragrance or put it by the entrance table to welcome guests.

Mix

15g (½oz) WHOLE CLOVES
2 CINNAMON STICKS (ROUGHLY BROKEN)
15g (½oz) ALLSPICE (WHOLE PIMENTO)

175g (6oz) DRIED ORANGE PEEL BROKEN INTO PIECES
10g (¼oz) DRIED ORANGE BLOSSOM OR BAY LEAVES

Orange Pomanders

*M*ake a basket of orange Pomanders; a traditional gift to give guests at Christmas when they leave.

About a month before, select fresh thin skinned oranges, lemons or apples. Using a tooth pick make holes about 5cm apart all over the fruit and stud with whole cloves. Mix 2 teaspoons of orris powder and 2 teaspoons of cinamon, and roll the fruit in the mixture. Wrap loosely in tissue and store in a dark place. Decorate with moss green velvet ribbon ties to hang.

Spiced Walnuts

*P*lace shelled walnut halves on a baking tray. Dot with butter and sprinkle with sugar and a little grated nutmeg. Bake at 350°F, 180°C or gas mark 4 for 10 to 15 minutes.

Buttery Almonds

*C*ombine almonds with a pinch of salt, dot with butter and toast under the grill. Be careful not to let them burn.

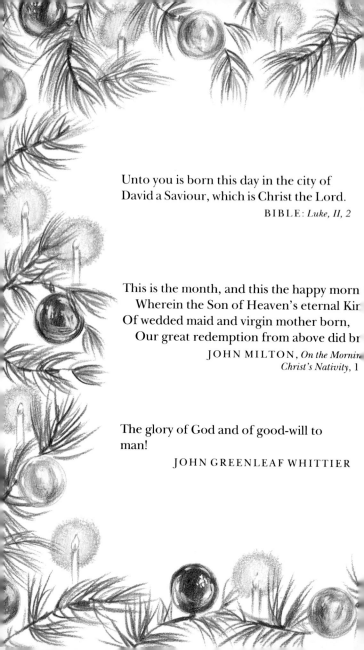

Unto you is born this day in the city of
David a Saviour, which is Christ the Lord.

BIBLE: *Luke, II, 2*

This is the month, and this the happy morn
  Wherein the Son of Heaven's eternal Kin
Of wedded maid and virgin mother born,
  Our great redemption from above did br

JOHN MILTON, *On the Mornin
Christ's Nativity,* 1

The glory of God and of good-will to
man!

JOHN GREENLEAF WHITTIER

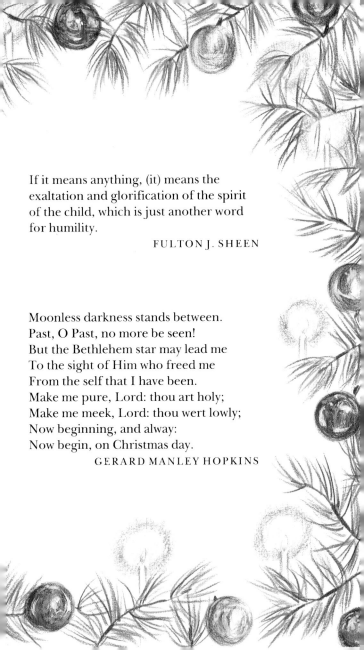

If it means anything, (it) means the
exaltation and glorification of the spirit
of the child, which is just another word
for humility.

FULTON J. SHEEN

Moonless darkness stands between.
Past, O Past, no more be seen!
But the Bethlehem star may lead me
To the sight of Him who freed me
From the self that I have been.
Make me pure, Lord: thou art holy;
Make me meek, Lord: thou wert lowly;
Now beginning, and alway:
Now begin, on Christmas day.

GERARD MANLEY HOPKINS

Christmas Eve, and twelve of the clock,
"Now they are all on their knees."
An elder said as we sat in a flock
By the embers in hearthside ease.

We pictured the meek mild creatures where
They dwelt in their strawy pen,
Nor did it occur to one of us there
To doubt they were kneeling then.

So fair a fancy few would weave
In these years! Yet, I feel,
If someone said on Christmas Eve,
"Come; see the oxen kneel

In the lonely barton by yonder coomb
Our children used to know",
I should go with him in the gloom,
Hoping it might be so.

THOMAS HARDY, *Oxen*

Christmas Cards

*C*hristmas cards first appeared in the mid-1800s. How eagerly we await the postman's delivery each day, for we know there will be Christmas cards. As each day draws nearer to Christmas the envelopes increase. All shapes and sizes, complete with postage stamps and seals announcing their own Christmas messages in miniature. Inside the blessings are varied but all convey the wish of happiness, and the hope that all that Christmas means may be preserved throughout the year; a simple way to share and give to those we care about.

You cannot reach
   perfection though
You try however
   hard to;
There's always one
   more friend or so
You should have sent
   a card to.

RICHARD ARMOUR

Christmas Paper Crackers

Simple paper crackers were popular in France before the invention of the "explosive" bon bon. Gold or silver paper was loosely wrapped around small candies and tied each end with ribbon. A tug at each end by two people until the cracker exploded scattered the candies on the floor and sent the children scrambling to pick them up.

Make some crackers to pile on a tray near the Christmas tree – friends can enjoy the fun of a tug-of-war for the sweets inside. A paper hat was always featured in the crackers of England and Australia. This was a relic of dressing-up in disguise at festivals. With imagination, all manner of surprises can be included in the cracker such as love messages, riddles, fans, flowers, tiny toys etc.

As a suggestion, start with 10 candies and two sheets of gold or silver gift wrap 150mm × 250mm (6″ × 10″). Overlap 12mm (1/2″) on the two 250mm (10″) edges and hold together with clear tape. Slip the candies into the centre. Twist each end of the paper, 75mm (3″) in from the end. Tie each twist with ribbon.

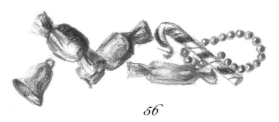

In Greece these cookies, heavily powdered with icing sugar and flavoured with almonds are a festive treat. A whole clove is stuck in the centre of each cookie to remind everyone of the spices brought by the Magi to the Christ Child. In Austria at Christmas-time these same cookies are shaped in a crescent.

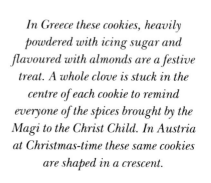

Courambiades

SHORTBREAD CHRISTMAS COOKIES

150g (5oz) FLOUR
PINCH SALT
155g (5oz) BUTTER
40g (1½oz) ICING SUGAR

2 EGG YOLKS
VANILLA
125g (4oz) GROUND
   ALMONDS
ICING SUGAR

Sift flour with salt onto a board. Make a well in the centre and put in butter, icing sugar, egg yolks and vanilla. Sprinkle ground almonds onto flour.

Work ingredients in centre with fingertips until thoroughly blended. Using a metal spatula, quickly draw in flour and ground almonds. Knead the dough lightly until smooth. Form the dough into a ball, wrap in greaseproof paper and chill for an hour.

Divide dough into small pieces and roll into balls the size of a small walnut, pinch top with thumb to shape into a pear. Push a whole clove into top as a stalk. Bake in a moderate oven, 350°F, 180°C or gas mark 4 for 10–12 minutes. Remove to a wire rack to cool, placing a sheet of paper underneath. Dredge biscuits heavily with sifted icing sugar while still warm. Cool.

On the twelfth day of Christmas, my true love
    sent to me
Twelve lords a-leaping, eleven ladies dancing,
Ten pipers piping, nine drummers drumming,
Eight maids a-milking, seven swans a-swimming,
Six geese a-laying, five gold rings,
Four colly birds, three French hens,
Two turtle doves and
A partridge in a pear tree.

A very merry Christmas, with roast beef in a violent perspiration, and the thermometer 110 in the shade! A remarkably merry Christmas, with the hot wind raging, and one's plate of Christmas cheer two fork-handles-deep in gravel! An excessively merry Christmas for John Shepherd, as he sits in the shade of his cabbage-tree hat on the burnt-up grass of the Tartarus Plains, and munches his bread and mutton wearily, while the sheep lie in panting groups, strung out under the haze. . . . It may be rank heresy, but I deliberately affirm that Christmas in Australia is a gigantic mistake.

MARCUS CLARKE, *Australasian, 26 December* 1868

Now every man at my request
Be glad and merry all in this fest.

Lett no man cum into this hall,
Grome, page, nor yet marshall,
But that sum sport he bryng withall;
For now is the time of Christymas!

At Christmas, when old friends are
   meeting,
We give that long-loved joyous
   greeting – "Merry Christmas!"
Though each land names a different
   name,
Good will rings through each with
   the same – "Merry Christmas!"
     DOROTHY BROWN THOMPSON

HERE IS A LIST OF CHRISTMAS
GREETINGS IN OTHER
LANGUAGES TO SHARE:

Kang Hsi Hsin Nien (Chinese)
Vesele Vanoce (Czechoslovakian)
Glaedelig Jul (Danish)
Zalig Kerstfeest (Dutch)
Joyeux Noel (French)
Frohliche Weihnachten (German)
Kala Christougena (Greek)
Kellemes Karacsonyi Unnepeket
(Hungarian)
Buon Natale (Italian)
Meri Kurisumasu (Japanese)
He Mere Kirihimete (Maori)
Bozego Narodzenie (Polish)
Feliz Natal (Portuguese)
Srozhdestvom Chrisstovym
(Russian)
Feliz Navidad (Spanish)
Glad Jul (Swedish)

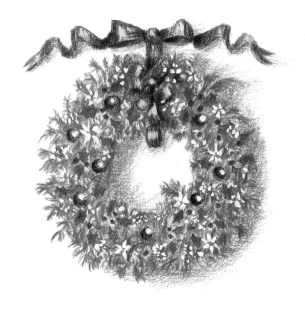

Merry Christmas